MW00366959

# COMFORTED

# FROM

# HEAVEN

*My travel to the Gates of Heaven and Back*

*Comforted From Heaven*
by C. Deanne Rowe

*Other Books by C. Deanne Rowe:*
Colt and Cassy
Southern Sophistication
Cowboy Owns Her Heart
Accidental Cowgirl
Alana's List
Remember Me
In the Heart of Valley
Return to Valley Dream of Valley
Dream of Valley
Secrets of Puckerbrush
Return to Puckerbrush
Beyond Puckerbrush

Copyright © March 2018 by C. Deanne Rowe

Cover Creation by Rebecca K. Sterling, Sterling Design Studios

All Rights Reserved. Except for use in any review, the reproduction or utilization of this book in whole or in part in any form, electronic, mechanical or other means, now known or hereafter invented, including photocopying and recording, or in any information storage or retrieval system, is forbidden without the written permission of the author, C. Deanne Rowe.

First Printing: March 2018

Printed in the United States of America

**ISBN-13: 978-1-946122-17-9**
ISBN-10: 1-946122-17-3

# DEDICATION

This book is dedicated to the Urbandale Iowa Fire Department Paramedics, the Doctors and Nurses of Iowa Methodist Trauma Center and the Doctors and Nurses of Iowa Methodist Critical Care Unit. Without your exceptional care and dedication to your profession, I would not be here to share my story.

# ACKNOWLEDGEMENTS

I struggled with the idea of writing this book, how to write it, what message should I leave with the people who read it? I wanted to know what happened to me and why, but there was also a part of me that didn't want to delve into the details. The wanting to know side won out. I wish to acknowledge the people who helped me get there.

My family, who endured and still endures endless questions and conversations about the events surrounding those days.

Maggie Rivers, my good friend and writing partner, who patiently gave me time, space and support to find the answers I needed. Also, the encouragement to use my writing skills and put my story down on paper.

Darrel Day, author and friend, who has also dealt with pulmonary embolisms and with his own near-death experience which hopefully he will share with all of you some day. Darrel, along with Maggie, gave me the support I needed to finish my story.

Mike Manno, Deacon, attorney and author, who took the time to listen to my story embellished with sobs and tears and then told me Jesus visited me and comforted me, which is where my title came from. He also encouraged me to write my story down.

Jesus Christ, my Lord and Savior, who never gave up on me. I gave my life to you as a young girl and you have been on my right side ever since. I've not always been the most obedient of servants, but you still showed me your unconditional love and comforted me when I needed you most.

# AUTHOR'S NOTE
## TWO YEARS LATER

I've decided now is the time for me to finish my story. If there ever was a time for inspiration, it would be now. I'm in a room filled with friends and fellow authors, each working on their current work in progress. These friends have been there with me and for me as I try to find my new normal. It's been two years and I'm still searching. What I'm searching for, I'm not really sure. There have been days of ups and days of downs. The ups have not been euphoric highs, but more of an ability to handle what the day brings. The downs have been so deep in the depths of despair I didn't know if I could or wanted to make it through.

The only way I can describe this feeling of being lost in your own reality is if you move into a new house bringing all your belongings with you. You are surrounded by familiar things, but the shell that holds them has changed. Everything belongs in a new place. Attempting to make places for what you know, what made you comfortable before, can prove impossible. This feeling can overwhelm you. Imagine waking to begin your day and knowing the responsibilities that lie in front of you don't hold the same fulfillment as they did before. You don't look forward to engaging in anything. You are just making it through your day, checking each responsibility off your list and retiring at night, wondering why and if you can do it again the next day. This is my day-to-day existence now. I know the only way to change this is to let go of everything I knew before, jumble them up like pieces of a puzzle. If they belong, they will fit back into place. If they don't, then it's time to let them go.

*Serenity Prayer - Lord, grant me the serenity to accept the things I cannot change, courage to change the things I can and the wisdom to know the difference. *

"No one can confidently say that he will still be living tomorrow,"—Euripides

In early April 2011, I stood at my patio door, taking in the beauty of the grass beginning to green; the trees beginning to bud. My three dogs were enjoying sniffing out all the scents which had reappeared from underneath the snow cover of winter.

Spring is my favorite time of the year. The world is coming alive after several months of freezing temperatures and cabin fever. This spring was one I was looking forward to and embracing the feeling that everything in my life was good. My family was growing, my job was fulfilling, and a dream of mine was coming true. In May 2011, my first book would be published. Two friends and I had each written a short story and we put them together in a novella titled 'Blue Jeans and Stilettos'. We had our first book signing coming up in the next month. All was right with the world. Or at least I thought. I had no idea how my world would change in the next few weeks. No one could have convinced me nothing would ever be the same.

My yearly mammogram was scheduled for the end of April. I was sure I would have a normal reading like all the others had been. I was wrong. The doctor saw something he didn't like, so I was scheduled for a second mammogram and an ultrasound. On Friday, April 13, 2011, I had a surgical biopsy because the spot they saw was too close to my chest wall to do a needle biopsy. On April 18, I waited to receive a call from my surgeon. Waiting until midafternoon, I still had heard nothing from his office, so I called. My world came crashing down. I thought someone had pulled the floor out from under me. I could hear him speaking, but all I remember him saying was Ductal carcinoma in situ (DCIS). I had cancer.

The next four months of my life were physically filled with doctor appointments, surgery, radiation treatments and more doctor appointments. Mentally, they were filled with questions about what was happening to my body. Would my body be disfigured? How would the radiation treatments affect me? I was determined to fight this disease, and I knew it would not be easy. Most of all was the fear of what my future held. Would this cancer come back?

As the next four years passed, with each doctor appointment and clear mammogram, my future was getting back to normal. I was released from my surgeon and my doctor appointments, which were scheduled for every six months, were now stretched out to once a year.

I decided with this new lease on life; it was time to take care of my knee. I had put my knee pain on hold during my recovery. I was in good health and it was becoming harder and harder to keep up with my grandchildren. It was time to make this change. After all, I had fought breast cancer and won. Knee surgery would be a breeze.

## SEPTEMBER 15, 2015

After many years of trying everything available to help with my knee pain, I decided to follow my orthopedic doctor's advice and have what seems to be a very common surgery, total knee replacement.

When telling my family my plans, I received mixed opinions. My husband supported my decision to have my knee replaced. My son Ryan, daughter-in-law Laci and daughter Sara had been asking me for several years when I was going to have my knee replaced. My son-in-law, Jace's mother, along with several co- workers, had their knees replaced and were doing great. My family knew I was having a hard time doing normal things and was in pain. My younger sister Lisa and my brother Mike were very uncomfortable with my decision. They didn't have a good feeling.

My husband and I attended a class on what to expect from my knee replacement surgery a week before my scheduled surgery date. We were two of the youngest people in the room. There was a woman attending with her daughter, who was planning to go directly into a rehab center as soon as they released her from the hospital because her daughter didn't have time to take off work to care for her. I felt blessed my husband had planned to take time from work to care for me. There was an older gentleman there with his two sons who was having both knees done. One on Monday and the other on the following Friday. I remember thinking if he could have both knees replaced within a week of each other, then I certainly could find the courage to have one knee replaced.

As they handed booklets out, all the information was covered, and questions were asked. I was scared, but stayed focused on how much better I would be after the surgery. With my pre-surgery physical done and my short-term disability approved, everything was in order.

The day of my surgery, my husband and I showed up at the registration department of the surgical hospital, filled out the necessary paperwork and waited to be called back to a room where I would be prepped for surgery.

It took a lot of mental preparation for me to summon the courage to go through with this surgery. All that preparation was failing me now. My breast cancer surgeries went fine and were necessary, so they were easier to accept. Replacing my knee was an elective surgery. Even though it was becoming more difficult to walk for any distance or sleep at night, this surgery was by choice. Walking through the mall was a feat in itself. I found myself more often than not staying home and shopping online or letting my husband have the pleasure of going with me, dropping me off at the closest door and then picking me up after we had finished shopping. He knew how much pain I was in, so he never complained. I think he was happy with the prospect of me being able to be active without moaning about my knee pain. This was going to be a good thing. At least I believed it would be.

After spending time with the surgical assistant in a private room the morning of my surgery going through all the pre-surgery routine, my surgeon entered the room. Looking professional in his white coat with his name over the pocket. He let me know he was prepared, asked me to tell him which knee he would operate on, and signed it with his initials. He asked if I was ready for surgery. I remember making some remark that I wasn't sure.

My surgeon made it clear if I wasn't sure I could leave. I didn't have to go through with the surgery. They could release me right then.

This was the one of many times in my life I ignored what I refer to now as heart whispers. Before I would refer to this feeling as intuition, instinctive feelings, hunches, inklings, sixth sense, gut reaction, internal nudges. Whatever you call it, my heart was telling me to listen to him and leave. My younger sister would tell me later she didn't have heart whispers, she had stomach pangs. She has gotten them her entire life when she didn't feel something was right. She told me she had talked to my brother Mike and Aunt Carol, telling them she didn't want me to have this surgery.

Of course, I didn't listen to my heart whispers or didn't know about my sister's stomach pangs. I had made all the arrangements, and I had convinced myself I was ready for this surgery. This surgery was going to solve my knee pain. I would be good as new in after a short recovery. At least that was what I was told in class and by my surgeon. I had no reason not to believe them. After all, friends and family members that had gone through this surgery and couldn't say enough about how much better their knee felt. I couldn't wait to say the same.

I woke in the recovery room, was taken to a private room, and moved into a hospital bed. The block they gave me before surgery was still working, so I was in no pain. My family was there to make sure I was all right. I rested as well as I could between the nurses floating in and out. After the block wore off later in the day, I was helped out of bed and taken for a short walk around the room. Each day I walked a little farther, venturing out into the hallway. The goal was for me to maneuver on crutches and to walk up and down the number of stairs it took for me to enter my house before I could go home. Two days later, I was home in my bed.

They released me from the hospital with prescriptions for pain medication, gabapentin, and 325 milligram aspirin, with instructions on how to take them. I also was instructed to move every few hours to prevent blood clots.

My husband had equipped our house for my recovery. Handles on the toilet, a shower chair and all the throw rugs picked up so I wouldn't fall as I maneuvered around on my crutches.

My husband felt comfortable he could return to work a few days a week and my son had lunch with me on the days I was home alone. I had a list of movies I wanted to watch, some writing I wanted to complete, and I now had the time to do just that.

I became concerned, though. No matter what I tried, the swelling in my leg would not go down. I called my surgeon's office and asked about the swelling. I was told to keep putting my leg higher than my heart several times a day and to take walks along with doing my exercises. The weather was still nice, so I began walking outside. I followed all the rules given to me by my surgeon during class and when I was released from the hospital. I changed positions as often as I could. Nothing was working. I was becoming very discouraged with the outcome of a surgery that was going to change my life for the better. I didn't know just how much my life would change.

When I felt able, my husband took me walking around the cul-de-sac. More often than not, neighbors asking about my surgery would stop us. We spent a lot of time talking and catching up on the neighborhood happenings. It felt good to be out in the sunshine and among the world.

At the follow-up visit with my surgeon, they gave me the same instructions concerning the swelling in my leg. I asked about physical therapy and was told if I thought I needed it and couldn't do the exercises myself, he would write me a script. I was discouraged and felt somehow I had failed as I walked out of his office with a script for physical therapy in hand. I knew I needed help.

I made the first available appointment with a physical therapist and waited a few weeks before I could begin. It was difficult to find a chair that was comfortable. I tried sitting in my gliding rocker and bend my knee as it rocked. There were several times I ended up in tears and stopped.

It was over a month since my surgery. The swelling in my leg kept me from doing much when I could begin therapy. I pushed myself and gave it my best shot. My therapists did all they could to help with the swelling, even using kinesio tape on my calf to help reduce the swelling.

I had never heard of kinesio tape before and thought there was no way this tape would make a difference. How could putting what looked like duct tape on my calf reduce the swelling? From what I understand, the tape's slight tug on the skin stimulates lymph vessels to open and collect more fluid so they keep the body's fluids in balance and release the toxins, proteins and excess fluid. All I knew was I was willing to try anything.

Monday, October 19th, was my third physical therapy appointment. I had appointments on Wednesday and Friday of the same week. I was scheduled to return to work on Monday, October 27th. I couldn't imagine how I was going to be able to sit at my desk for eight hours a day with my leg swelling like it was. I had contacted the administrators of my short-term disability to request an extension, hoping for a few more weeks for the swelling to lessen and would give me the confidence I was doing the right thing.

# OCTOBER 23, 2015

Can you remember what you were doing on Friday, October 23, 2015? I can. This is one day I'll remember for the rest of my life. I even have an event created on my phone by my son for this day titled Second Life. This is why.

I woke to a day which was dreary and rainy but one filled with plans. My mother had flown in to visit for a few weeks. I had an appointment with my physical therapists that afternoon. Until then, I could spend some time with my mother.

Gathering clothing items for my shower, I placed them on the bathroom cabinet. I remember little of this morning, but I seem to recall having problems breathing. Making my way back to the bed to pick up the home phone, I first sat on the edge. Unable to control my body, I slid from the edge of the bed. I must have blacked out before I reached the floor.

The next I remember is lying on the floor and my mother telling me she didn't know what to do and asking for my husband's cell phone number. I don't remember seeing anything. Everything was black, but I could hear my mother's voice. Somehow, I gave her his number. She called him on her cell phone.

He instructed her to pick up the home phone and call 911. I don't remember any of their conversation. I must have blacked out again. In another of my lucid moments, she told me she had called for help. I thought to ask her to unlock the front door, so the responders didn't break it down. It's amazing how your mind works in time of trauma. I wanted to get up off the floor, but I couldn't feel my body. It was as if my mind and body were separate. There was no connection.

My mother had flown in on Tuesday, October 20th, planning to stay until the end of the month. Later, she would tell me she had considered cancelling her visit. She doesn't like cold weather and snow. She prayed about it and couldn't shake the feeling she needed to be here with me. That morning Mom was downstairs and heard my tea cup toy poodle, Allie, barking. She came upstairs to find out what Allie was barking about. Allie greeted her at the top of the stairs, still barking. Thinking I was still asleep, my mother believed Allie was telling her she needed to go outside. She convinced Allie to follow her to the back door, but she wasn't able to unlock the door. She didn't want to wake me, but she needed to ask me about the door. That's when she found me collapsed on the floor. Mom later told me the first thing she thought was to say a prayer over me from John 11: 1-44, The 6TH Sign: The Resurrection of Lazarus* reminding God he had brought Lazarus from the dead. She asked him to do the same for me.

If Mom had given in to her first thoughts of visiting and not come, my husband would have found me on the floor when he returned home from work.

My husband, Craig, and I were high school sweethearts. We married the summer I graduated. I worked and attended college part-time while my husband finished his degree. We basically grew up together. I can't image him coming home to find me lying on the bedroom floor. I am so grateful that didn't happen. Thank the good Lord for his blessings. I now know He placed so many people in my path to help me on this journey. One of those people was my mother.

When I woke again, I remember one paramedic asking me which hospital I wanted to be taken to. I replied "Iowa Methodist". I remember nothing more of this day. All I know for sure is it was a day I'll never forget. You see, it was the day I died.

# MEDICAL TIMELINE

I ordered a copy of my medical records and read through them, all 1,414 pages, in an attempt to help me piece together what happened during the five days I lost. The records include entries from Doctors, Nurses and chaplains. I am including pieces of those records below and including Caringbridge* posts my son, Ryan, made during this time. Sharing pieces of these records has helped me understand what my family has been telling me so I could begin to put together all the pieces I was missing. This is where it began as I arrived at Iowa Methodist Medical Center by ambulance.

Arrival Date/Time:      10/23/15 9:37 AM
Admission Type:         Emergency
Means of Arrival:       Ambulance
Admission Date/Time:    10/23/15 9:38 AM

1. Cardiac arrest
2. Metabolic acidosis
3. Pulmonary embolus, presumptive

Chief Complaint

Respiratory Distress

Patient is a 59-year-old female who presents to the ED with the complaints of cardiac arrest. According to paramedics, patient was found by family on the floor complaining of shortness of breath. Medics state that she was responsive to just prior to arrival. Patient arrived and respiratory distress and unresponsive to painful stimuli. She was unable to aid in history. Family states that the patient has a history of breast cancer and had knee surgery 5 weeks ago. Husband states that she has not had any complaints recently.

CRITICAL CARE TIME

There was a high probability of clinically significant life-threatening deterioration in the patient's condition which required my urgent intervention total critical care time with this patient was 95 minutes excluding separately reportable procedures.

Diagnoses: ACUTE CORONARY SYNDROME, CHRONIC OBSTRUCTIVE PULMONARY DISEASE, CONGESTIVE HEART FAILURE, PERICARDIAL TAMPONADE, PNEUMONIA,

PNEUMOTHORAX, PULMONARY EMBOLISM, SEPSIS, and THORACIC DISSECTION.

FINAL IMPRESSION

4. Cardiac arrest

5. Metabolic acidosis

6. Pulmonary embolus, presumptive

# TIMELINE OF TREATMENT
## 10/23/15

9:38 – Compression resumed. Patient bagged

9:39 - Compressions stopped. Femoral pulse located

9:46 - attempting intubation and was unsuccessful. RT resume bagging patient

9:47 - attempt intubation x2

9:48 - Positive $CO_2$ color change, bilateral breath sounds on both sides

9:51 - No pulse felt. Compressions started by Lucas device

9:54 - Compressions stopped for rhythm check. Pulses present

9:59 - EKG completed

10:04 - Pulse lost. CPR resumed by Lucas device

10:08 - CPR stopped for pulse check. Femoral pulses felt

10:17 - Pulses lost. CPR started

10:19 - CPR paused for rhythm check. Patient sinus tach with palpable femoral pulses

10:21 - Patient placed on ventilator 10:25 - Pulses lost. CPR resumed

10:25 - Pulses lost. CPR resumed

10:27 - CPR stopped for pulse check. Femoral pulses present

10:32 - 20 mg TPA IV push given

10:33 - 30 mg TPA given IV push

10:36 - <u>Femoral pulses lost. CPR initiated by Lucas Device</u>

10:39 - CPR stopped for pulse check. No pulses present. Patient in PEA (pulseless electrical activity). CPR resumed

10:42 - Husband at bedside

10:44 - CPR stopped for pulse check. Femoral pulses present

11:15 - Verbal order by Dr. for OG and foley placement

11:34 - TPA infusion finished

11:35 - Rhino rocket placed in right nostril

11:44 - Son and Husband at bedside

12:08 PM - ECHO at bedside

12:23 PM – Patient opening eyes, and bringing arms towards ETT (endotracheal tube). Propofol drip to be started

10/24/15
*ICU Day two*

A scan confirmed I had massive blood clots in each lung.
I also had a nosebleed for which an Ear, Nose Throat
Doctor was consulted. He placed nasal packing in each
nostril. It was also found I was anemic, which required
several units of packed red blood cells. I was diagnosed
with acute kidney injury for which I was given
continuous renal replacement therapy (CRRT) which is
used to treat critically ill, hospitalized patients in the
intensive care unit.
I also had a problem with anxiety. The goal was for me
to demonstrate the ability to manage my anxiety
effectively. I was not progressing. I became agitated or
anxious and very tense and rigid when I was turned or
oral care was attempted. My blood pressure would drop
below acceptable parameters. It would take me a while
to calm down and relax.

****

10/25/15
*ICU Day three*

My condition hadn't changed. My family was visited every day by the Hospital Chaplains. This day the Chaplain noted the following about her visit:

*Met with various family in the CCU waiting area during regular rounds. Prayed with them for continued healing and inspired care of Carla. Offered continued care as needed.*

****

10/26/15

*ICU Day four*

I remained sedated, on mechanical ventilation, and on continuous renal replacement therapy. The nurses noted I was more responsive this day. I was writing notes to my family.

My family also had another visit from one of the hospital chaplain. She noted the following in her report:

*Epic consult. Husband told me of patient's knee replacement 5 weeks earlier and welcomed prayer. He was sitting with his wife.*

****

10/27/15

*ICU Day five*

I didn't have to concern myself with returning to work on October 27th. Below is the first post from my daughter-in-law, Laci, on Facebook. The other are posts to a CaringBridge* site my daughter-in-law created and where my son, Ryan, posted to help keep family and friends updated on my condition. The first post was dated four days after I died. Since these days are totally lost for me, I have to rely on my family's memory and medical records to piece these days together.

Laci - October 27, 2015

*We love you so much, Deanne! You keep fighting and we'll keep praying!*

Mom

By Ryan — Oct 27, 2015 9:25am

As some of you may know, my mom's life took a surprising turn on Friday, October 23rd. She suffered a pulmonary embolism and narrowly escaped losing her life. We give thanks to and praise God for sparing her and giving her a fighting chance to live. It's extremely hard for us to understand why this happened to her, but we are leaving her healing in God's hands. She has numerous clots in her lungs as well as her legs. She has a very long road to recovery, so please pray for her. Please pray for comfort, strength and peace for our mom. She did make some small improvements yesterday and started dialysis, which her body responded well to. She was more alert yesterday and even let it be known I needed to stop reading to her!

She was even able to listen to her oldest grandchildren say "I love you" over the phone. The fantastic nurses and doctors are trying to keep her comfortable at this time, which has mostly meant keeping her sedated.

Every precious response we get from her leaves us happy and hopeful.

Romans 8:38

*And I am convinced that nothing can ever separate us from God's love. Neither death nor life, neither angels nor demons, neither our fears for today nor our worries about tomorrow-not even the powers of hell can separate us from God's love.*

****

October 27th

By Ryan — Oct 27, 2015 8:00pm

Just wanted to give everyone a quick update. Mom seems to be in good spirits, all things considered. She was very alert earlier today and enjoyed seeing us. She was even actively watching the Food Network (her favorite channel) with dad when I showed up. The dialysis has been going great and her blood pressure continues to improve even while they 'turn up' the dialysis treatment, which is good. She has also been given a feeding tube today, so she has steady stream of 'liquid cheeseburger' as the nurse called it.
She's still in critical condition and she still has a lot of meds and a breathing tube, so we're still hour to hour. That said, it's been a good day and we continue to pray for the healing of her body and peace in her mind during this process.

*1 Peter 5:7 cast all your anxiety on him because he cares for you.*

****

10/28/15

ICU Day six

The nurses noted I was more cooperative, responsive, and nodding yes/no to questions since I was still intubated. There was a promise my breathing tube would be removed today. My nose was still packed. My family was at my bedside as they had been each day. I was feeling better and my husband was relieved enough to begin joking with me.

****

October 28th - another good day

By Ryan — Oct 28, 2015 3:01pm

Mom has made some positive progress today, which is very welcomed by all of us. She's still critical and still has some clotting in her lungs and legs. They have been able to give her blood thinners again to try and treat the clots, so we continue to pray for the healing of her body to clear these out. The positives of the day are many! She has had her medications reduced significantly, her vitals have all remained strong, and she has had her breathing tube removed. The last item being the best news for her comfort of mind and body. She's said a little bit to us, but we're still trying to get her to rest her throat and keep her oxygen levels strong. We have loved hearing her hoarse voice though and look forward to hearing it more. For all that know my dad, he's been feeling good enough and happy enough to pick at my mom and she's paid him back with a flip of the bird. I've never been so happy to see sign language profanity in my life. It's the little things, you know?

*Psalm 46:1-3 God is our refuge and strength, a very present help in trouble. Therefore, we will not fear though the earth gives way, though the mountains be moved into the heart of the sea, though its waters roar and foam, though the mountains tremble at its swelling. Selah.*

****

10/29/15
*ICU Day seven*

October 29th - still trending upward
By Ryan — Oct 29, 2015 11:48am

It has been a very positive morning for mom. Her "beans" (kidneys) responded so well to dialysis that the doctors are giving her a day off. She'll still require dialysis treatments for the foreseeable future, but this is much better than 24/7 treatment. She has also been relieved of almost all of her IV's and meds. She's still on blood thinners, of course, but having her arms free for the most part has made mom very happy. She's carried on some very short yet enjoyable conversations with us today, and we've had some good laughs. She also gets to eat some actual food today for the first time since Thursday, which is an amazing sign to me. Overall, things are progressing very well and we are so thankful. I personally want to thank everyone for their kind words, their thoughts, and their prayers. They have all been helpful during this time and I appreciate that they will continue as mom continues to heal. Thank you.
Romans 15:13 May the God of hope fill you with all joy and peace in believing, so that by the power of the Holy Spirit you may abound in hope.

****

The nurses noted I was much more alert today. It was also the day my nose packs would be removed. I could begin to attempt to breathe through my nose again. There was talk of moving me from ICU to the rehabilitation floor.

****

10/30/15

*ICU Day eight*

Add your comments here
By Ryan — Oct 30, 2015 10:39am

Mom is doing well enough that we have been reading the posts and comments gathered here, and she has enjoyed every one of them. Thank you so much! So, if you'd like to direct anything to mom in the comments sections (well wishes, prayers, jokes, verses, etc.) have at it and we'll be sure to read them to her later today. Thanks!

****

10/31/15

The Floor Day One

Moving Day

By Ryan — Oct 31, 2015 4:30pm

First off, thank you all so much for all of your kind
words. My mom has read or heard all of your messages
and each one has lifted her spirits. It's been great to
interact with her more every day in the ICU, but late last
night she made the move from ICU to "the floor". Her
new room is in the rehabilitation center of Methodist.
This move means that amazing progress has been made
and I hope that it continues. Considering where she was
a week ago, this was a huge relief and mighty victory.
After the move, she slept well and looked really great
this morning when we went to visit her. Selfishly, I was
relieved that Alexa and Alivia were finally able to see
Grandma. They dressed up in their Halloween costumes
(Alivia as Minnie Mouse and Alexa as Dorothy from
Wizard of Oz) and were nothing short of ecstatic to see
their grandma for the first time in over a week. It was a
good day. Mom still has a long road to recovery but
we're going to celebrate this victory. Happy Halloween
everyone!

****

## 11/1/15
### *The Floor Day Two and Three*

The next few days, I was adjusted to a regular stream of new faces floating in and out of my room. The nurses taking my stats and doctors who were taking over my care from the doctors in ICU. I could also have visitors other than family. It was exhausting but good to be able to feel I was joining the world again.

The doctors and nurses wanted me to move around more. It took a team to move me out of the bed. I still had central lines on each side of my neck and a catheter. They moved a chair beside my bed so I could sit up while eating lunch and dinner. I began slowly, but sitting on the edge of my bed a few times a day. Trying to brush my own teeth and manage the simplest of tasks.

****

## 11/3/15
### *The Floor Day Three*

Quick update
By Deanne — Nov 3, 2015 9:24pm

I decided I'm getting strong enough to give my son, Ryan, a break from making journal entries and make one myself. I wanted to thank all of you for your outpouring of affection. I knew God had blessed me with great friends. I just didn't know how great. I continue to improve every day, but I'm still not sure what the future holds. One thing I do know is I have the most beautiful family. My mom, my sisters, their families, my brother and his family, my aunts and uncles, four beautiful grandkids, a wonderful significant other for my daughter, the most precious daughter-in-law, two of the most loving kids a mother could ask for and a loving husband who almost never left my side. My heart swells with pride. I'm one lucky woman to be given another chance to spend time with all of them. As soon as I'm better, I owe my son one long conversation.

\*\*\*\*

## 11/4/15
### The Floor Day Four

My INR had been trending up nicely, but not yet where the doctors wanted it to be. I was beginning to feel the effects of what had happened to me. My entire body ached. My legs from my knee surgery and also from the blood clots. I was to begin Physical Therapy today. Today I received a visit from one of the Hospital Chaplains. My husband was in the room with me. I couldn't help but notice how he had become acquainted with the Chaplains enough to recognize them.

The following was the Chaplain's notes about his visit with us:

*I stopped to visit with the patient and her husband while making rounds on Y-8. It was difficult for the patient to speak, so her husband did most of the talking. They told me about her arrival in the emergency room a week ago Friday and the blood clots in both of her lungs. They were both very thankful that the patient had healed as much as she has. I prayed for continued healing for her.*

\*\*\*\*

11/5/15
*The Floor Day Five*

This was my night for a sleep study. Since I was captive, my pulmonologist call for the sleep study to come to me instead of me having to go to it. I was becoming more mobile and going home was not far away. My central lines were removed, which made it possible for me to shower in the next day or so.

**\*\*\*\***

## 11/6/15
### *The Floor Day Six*

Today was a great day. I had my catheter removed. I was mobile. Everything still tasted funny, but I could move around more and the swelling in my legs was going down. I was ready to take a shower and be discharged.

**\*\*\*\***

## 11/8/15
### *Home*

By Ryan — Nov 8, 2015 4:53 pm

Hello all - I apologize for the lack of updates as of late. As you saw with the last update, mom was able to post her thanks and I'm sure that was a welcome sign to all. Throughout this past week, mom's body continued to heal to the point where she had all IV's and ports removed on Thursday evening. The removal of the ports means that her kidneys repaired themselves well enough that dialysis will not be something that she needs to worry about going forward. Most importantly, the removal of all this equipment allowed her to be discharged to the comfort of her own home on Saturday afternoon! She's still pretty weak and tired, so she will have regular visits from nurses and physical therapists to ensure that she's still progressing with her healing. But being able to be at home is very much a blessing for her and my dad. Thank you all again for the prayers sent mom's way and she very much appreciates all those kind and uplifting words.

Psalm 30:2 - "O Lord my God, I cried to you for help, and you have healed me,"

# MY ICU STAY
## *My point of view*

I learned later a prayer chain had been started for me as soon as my mother found me collapsed on the floor. I'm not sure who she called first but my older sister and her family began a prayer chain in Tennessee, my younger sister began a prayer chain in North Carolina, my older brother began a prayer chain in Colorado and my Aunt began one in Oklahoma. My son and daughter-in-law began a prayer chain at their church and their workplaces.

My writing partner, Maggie, began a prayer chain at the writing retreat I was supposed to attend that weekend. She sent emails and created a post on Facebook asking for prayers from our friends and also all of our fans who follow our writing career. Other members of the group also created posts. It amazes me to know how many people these posts touched.

Some of my co-workers began praying as soon as they learned what happened. One even asked his son to offer petitions for me at Benedictine College. I had prayers coming from Tennessee, Alabama, Mississippi, North Carolina, Colorado, Oklahoma, Arizona, Nebraska,

California and Des Moines. When I think of how many prayers were being said for me, it is humbling and amazing. I told a friend I believe God heard my name so many times in prayer he couldn't keep me in heaven. He had to send me back.

My younger sister would tell me later that on Sunday after I collapsed on Friday, she and her husband, Alan, were in Charlotte, North Carolina, attending a Panthers football game. They were preparing to drive to Des Moines that next day if they felt they needed to. When she woke up that Sunday morning, she felt a relief in her heart and she shared that with Alan. When she talked to our brother, she told him I was going to be okay and that my kidneys would begin to function again.

The prayers worked and I guess losing five days is a fair exchange for not losing my life. I know in those lost five days I was lifted up in prayer and I was where God needed me to be.

I woke, not knowing what had happened to me or where I was. I remember trying to move my hands to feel what was on my face, but my hands were tied to the bed I was laying in. I couldn't talk. I had been intubated and my nose had been packed. My husband was talking to me and my son was reading me messages and emails from friends. I was trying to understand why. There were pictures of two of my grandchildren taped to the wall beside the bed so I could see them when my eyes were open. Why couldn't I move? Why couldn't I talk? All I could do was cry. My daughter had to wipe my tears.

My last memory was being at home. Collapsing beside the bed. I had no clue where I was, how I got there, and how serious things were. Waking in Intensive Care, not knowing why, when or how you got there or what day it is, can be a horribly frightening experience.

My family was there at all times to try and keep me calm during when I was conscious. My grandson, Kael, was allowed to visit me in ICU. He was the only one of my grandchildren considered old enough. I remember him holding my hand so tightly with such a look of concern as he told me he loved me. My heart broke. I could only imagine what this ten-year-old boy was feeling and thinking. Whether it was the sedation or my family keeping me calm, I'm not sure how I managed. I wanted to go home. I didn't want to be there. I knew in my heart I would have never accepted being intubated if I had been conscious.

I am still trying to piece together the days I lost with my families' memories and what they are willing to talk to me about. It has taken time for each of them to begin to tell me what they remember because, for them, it is as raw a memory as it is for me. Reliving these moments is something none of them wish to do.

My son and daughter-in-law have been very helpful filling me in with what they could manage to tell me. My husband carefully tells me in bits and pieces when he feels it is the right time for me to know. The same with my daughter. I've tried to be understanding even though I would love to have all the pieces to connect. I don't know how well I would have done dealing with what was happening if our places had been changed. I thank the good Lord it was me in this situation and not one of them, so I don't have to find out.

Not sure whether the trauma my body had suffered had caused heart or brain damage, they performed an MRI, which showed nothing. My mind began to work, which was a huge relief to my husband, but not being able to speak because of the breathing tube, I tried to write notes to my family. My husband did his best to interpret what I was scribbling, and most of the time he did well. Other times, he needed help from my son and daughter to understand. He kept every one of the notes I had scribbled to him. I look at them now and then to remind me how far I've come, just like I re-read the CaringBridge* posts to try and remember.

I don't recall being as much concerned about why I was in ICU as I was the following concerns which I attempted to write notes for my husband and children to interpret. It was difficult to write because my hands were tied to the bed rail. My first request was to make the ties longer.

Can you make Them longer

My next concern was my jewelry. I couldn't remember if I was wearing any jewelry when I was taken to the hospital. I could feel a piece of metal by my thumb on my right hand. This is the thumb which I wear my father's wedding ring. My father passed away in July 2000 and as my brother, sisters and I cleaned out his house, I found two rings packed away in the back of a closet. My younger sister took one, and I took the other. I wear his ring almost every day. Feeling the metal, I was afraid they had cut the ring off my finger. I didn't want to lose it. I remember thinking if I had to, I would have it repaired.

My husband assured me my jewelry was safe at home. I couldn't get him to understand about the metal by my thumb. Every time I woke, I felt for the piece of metal to make sure it was still safe. Later, I would find out it was a port the doctors had put in my vein because they kept collapsing. My father's ring was safe at home in my jewelry box, just as my husband had told me.

money Rings

Ring

Ring

My ICU nurse suggested to my husband that he call the surgeon who had performed my knee surgery and let him know what had happened to me. I remember waking to my surgeon standing over my bed talking to my husband. I still had my breathing tube and my nose packed. He pulled my sheet back and looked at my knee. I remember him saying how my knee looked beautiful and he could fix my mobility problem when I got out of ICU. Since I couldn't speak, I looked at my husband and shook my head no. The thought of him touching me again made me physically ill. For all I knew, he was the reason I was in ICU.

I don't remember what I was trying to tell my husband. I'll I know is that it upset me my surgeon was there. Neither one of us could interpret what I was trying to write.

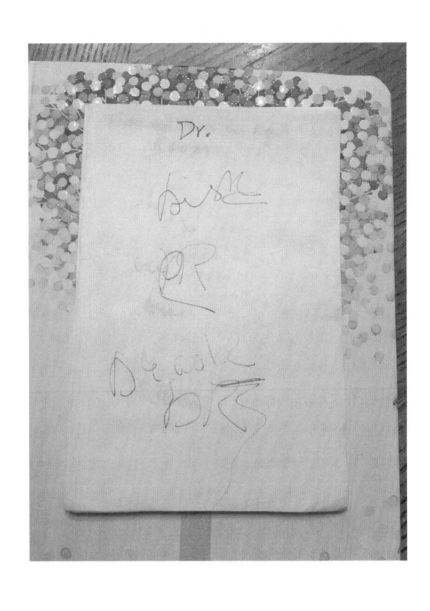

Another concern was contacting the company who was handling my short-term disability claim. I knew my claim had ended the Monday I was to return to work.

The last thing I needed, along with being in ICU, was worrying whether or not my short-term disability would be extended. My husband assured me he had called the company and everything was fine.

The bugs were next on my list. I remember seeing little black bugs crawling up the walls and disappearing into the ceiling. At one point, the bugs were on my bed sheets and on my husband's shirt. My husband finally understood I wanted him to shake my sheets to get rid of the bugs. He tried his best to convince me there were no bugs as he shook my sheets. I could still see bugs no matter how hard he tried to tell me they weren't there. I remember closing my eyes and telling myself over and over there were no bugs. My husband assured me there were no bugs, so there were no bugs. Right.

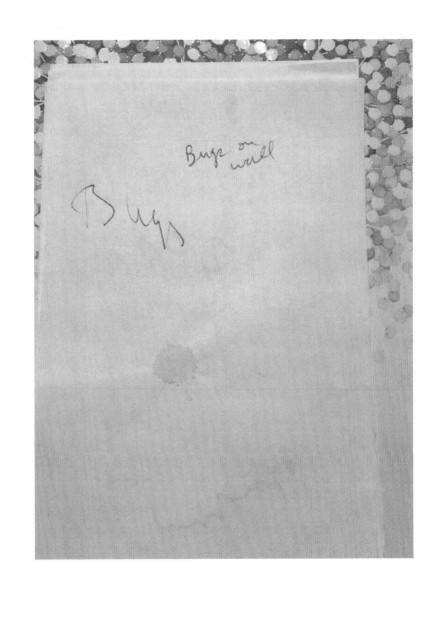

Bugs on wall

Bugs

Shake

Shake

Bugs

As my husband talked to the nurses about the bugs, he also talked to them about me seeing a man in my room. The nurses were not concerned at all about the man in my room, but they were concerned about the bugs. They told my husband there couldn't have been a man in my room because there were no male nurses working at night and no male doctors had been in to check on me at night. The bugs were a concern because it meant my medications were off. Something wasn't right, so they had to make some adjustments.

At some point, my husband told me they needed to give me blood. I don't know why I didn't trust the professionals to find my blood type and make sure I received the correct type, but I had to make sure they knew I was 0 negative. I remember my husband assuring me they knew my blood type and it would be all right.

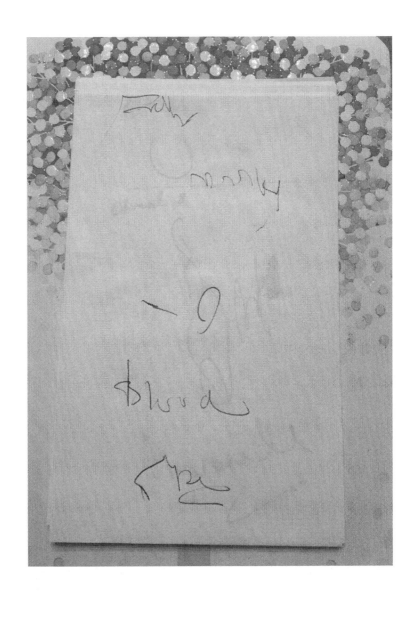

I was still concerned with a man being in my room at night. If he wasn't a doctor or nurse, who was he? I was in complete darkness. There was a man dressed in white standing next to me on my right side. At the end of the darkness was a circle of light. In the light were people milling around. They seemed to being going on about their lives as if nothing was wrong. It reminded me of when my mother would leave the hallway light on at night, so my sisters and I wouldn't be afraid to go to sleep. This light was much brighter and intense.

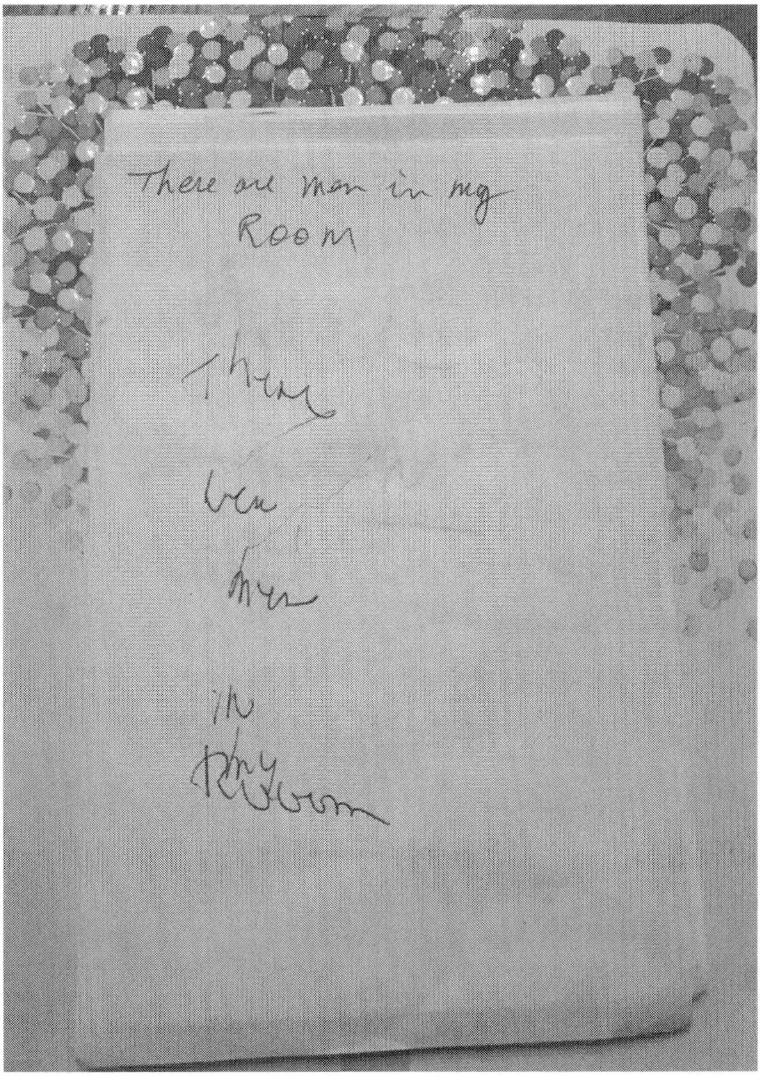
There are man in my
Room

As I tried to focus on the man standing next to me, his face became clearer. I had a strange feeling of not so much fear as despair. As his face came into focus, I believed I had been kidnapped by a Klingon. I was on a spaceship and they were taking me far away from my family. I remember my heart being so heavy with sadness, as if I had lost someone close and dear to me. The thought of never seeing my husband, children, and grandchildren was almost too much for me to bear.

As my despair grew, a hand touched my right arm. His face became even clearer. He had long, stringy brown hair and the blackest eyes I have ever seen. I could feel the calm. He spoke to me, but I don't remember his mouth moving. I could hear him say, "You have to fight, Deanne. We'll take care of you."

My next memory was waking in ICU with my husband and son standing beside my bed.

\*\*\*\*

Still not being able to talk and knowing I wasn't able to write down all I wanted to say, I decided I would wait until I could go tell my family about being kidnapped by a Klingon. My husband had managed to make out my scribbles, but I wouldn't be able to get him to understand this. After writing him a short note, he asked me if I was trying to tell him there were men in my room. When I let him know he was right, he never left my side at night. He slept in a chair in my room, only leaving when another family member was there so he could shower, change clothes and try to sleep a few hours at home.

My daughter had come to the hospital after work to relieve my husband. He was so exhausted that he slept longer than he planned. My daughter needed to go home, so against her better judgment, she left for home, leaving me alone. I would later find out she cried all the way home because she didn't want to leave me alone.

I'm almost positive this is the night I was, what I believed then, to be kidnapped. I've heard stories of people who wait to pass until they are alone so their family doesn't have to witness their death.

Every time I woke for the next several days, there was a family member beside my bed. When they realized I was awake, they would tell me what day it was and what time of day it was. Later I found out they had been told people in ICU could develop what was called ICU Dementia. Trying everything they could to try and help me heal, they took it upon themselves to do whatever they could to prevent whatever they could from happening to me. I just thought they were trying to irritate me by informing me how long I had been in ICU and how nothing was changing. Oh, ye of little faith!

****

The day I was asked if I would like to have my breathing tube removed, I couldn't nod my head yes in agreement enough times. I wanted to be able to speak instead of attempting to write notes. My family had no idea what they were in for. I wanted to have my hands untied from the bed. As the nurses began to trust I wouldn't pull my breathing tube, they loosened my hands a little to give me more movement.

That trust was almost lost the only night I remember trying to pull my breathing tube because I couldn't get the nurse's attention. My husband informed me it wasn't the first time I had tried. I realized now what a stupid move that was. In my defense, they had given me a stool softener earlier in the day. It had begun to take effect. A nurse was nowhere to be found. I did not know where the call button was and I couldn't get my husband's attention. The only solution in my drug crazed mind was to try to pull my breathing tube. Not only did I get their attention, but did I get a lecture not only from the nurse but also from my husband.

The next thing I remember was the night nurse, in a stern but concerned voice, telling me, "Carla, you can't be doing that. I'm going to have to tie your hands back if we can't trust you to not try to pull your tube."

I acknowledged her request and let her know I needed a bedpan. After everything was taken care of, I drifted back off to sleep or wherever it was I went when I wasn't present. She apologized to me later for the stool softener and I apologized for trying to pull my tube. We both forgave and forgot.

Now it was time to take out the breathing tube for good. It couldn't happen fast enough. I wanted this foreign thing out of my body. They would stop having to clean the tube and swabbing my teeth.

It only took a few seconds for them to remove the tube, but my nose packing remained. As soon as the tube was gone, an oxygen mask was placed on my face. I wanted nothing else on my face, but the mask was much easier to accept than a tube down my throat. Removal of my breathing tube also meant they could untie my hands from the bed. I had more freedom, but I still was very weak and had trouble moving. I would still have to be rolled side to side to change sheets, change my gown or use the bedpan.

One instance when using the bedpan, my favorite male nurse, Dave, asked another male nurse for help rolling me on my side. It was routine for Dave seeing me in all my glory. After a few days in ICU, you lose all inhibitions. This new male nurse was very attractive. I could only see him from the waist up, but he looked as if he was very fit. I joked with Dave that he needed to find another assistant because this new nurse was too 'pretty'. I remember the disappointed look on Dave's face and his response. "What am I? Chopped liver?" My Stiletto Girl story telling came into play. Maggie would be proud. I assured him that I loved him and this new nurse was just eye candy. We all had a good laugh, which was becoming a way for me to pass time. I was happy I hadn't lost my sense of humor.

After the doctor removed my breathing tube and everyone left the room, the first thing I told my husband and son was about being kidnapped by a Klingon. After managing with labored breathing to explain to them what I remember, my son's eyes grew as big as silver dollars. I tried to make them understand. I knew it sounded strange, but I told them exactly what I remembered. I was so sure I was giving them each little detail and letting them know how real it was to me.

Not wanting to upset me, they listened and smiled, believing every word. Later, I would learn how crazy I must have sounded.

****

On my last day in ICU, I managed to eat food on my own. I was going to be moved to the rehabilitation wing of the hospital. I learned in order for this to happen, I had to be able to eat, sit in a chair and have my kidney function improve.

It was painful to do the simplest of movements. I found out later they had cracked my sternum when the paramedics, doctors and nurses were performing CPR.

Two nurses helped me out of my bed and into a nearby chair. It took both of them and a safety belt around my waist to move me. I remember how exhausting it was to just sit up. I was in tears by the time they had sat me down in the chair.

My daughter was in the room with me and was becoming increasingly irritated with one nurse as she kept telling me I had to 'work through the pain'. How she had twisted her knee, and she had to make herself work through the pain. I was proud of my daughter. She kept her cool and listened to her story.

When she left the room, my daughter began to rant how she could possibly compare twisting her knee to what I was going through. It was as if we had changed places and she was protecting me. It was a wonderful thing to witness. If I had felt any sense of normal, I would have laughed.

I stayed sitting in the chair until the nurses decided it was time for me to be put back in bed. The idea of moving again brought me to tears again, but the thought of staying sitting up in the chair was the worse of two evils. I made the move and could finally get back into bed, hoping the small amount of food I had managed to eat would stay down.

They brought dialysis to me instead of me being taken to dialysis. A huge machine was hooked up and ran for about half an hour before they could begin.

During one day I lost, they had surgically inserted two central lines in my neck, one on each side. The left side was used for blood draws and administering medication. The port on the right was used for dialysis. During the days I lost, I was on dialysis twenty-four hours a day. Dialysis is the artificial replacement for lost kidney function. As my kidneys began working better, I was taken off and given a break.

Before I would be able to leave ICU, I needed to receive one more dialysis treatment.

After they hooked me up to the machine, it took four hours to complete this one session. I can't imagine having to go through this procedure every day. I gained a new empathy for people who have to go through dialysis to be able to survive. The nurse who administered the dialysis treatment stayed with me the entire time, making sure the procedure was going as it should. I felt sorry for her. I was so tired I snored through the entire process, waking myself up several times.

I was allowed to rest for a few hours after dialysis before they gave me a bath. One of the ICU nurses brought in all the necessary equipment and bathed me like a mother would a child. She took such care to make sure my body was clean; I was wearing deodorant and my teeth were brushed. The only thing she couldn't do was wash my hair because of the central lines placed in my neck.

I was so exhausted when she finished I remember nothing until I was told I was being moved to a room on the eighth floor of the rehabilitation wing. I was happy, and I was also scared.

## MOVING TO REHABILITATION WING

Leaving ICU meant I was physically doing better.

It meant I was stable, which gave my husband the courage to tell me what had happened to me. I remember him standing at the end of my hospital bed asking me if I wanted to know. I agreed, and he began to tell me how I died and they brought me back. He proceeded to tell me I had massive blood clots in both lungs and in my legs. When I arrived at the emergency room, I coded. The doctors and nurses managed to bring me back, only to lose my pulse five more times. The last time I coded, my husband and son were in the room.

They had worked on me for ninety-five minutes. The doctors were looking at my husband, waiting for him to tell them to stop, and they were about to call the time of death when one doctor found a faint femoral pulse, which I managed to maintain. I was in critical condition and it was minute to minute whether I would survive.

Also, the fear that I had gone too long without oxygen and whether blood clots had caused any damage to my heart or brain. My husband was very concerned because several times the nurses asked if I knew who my husband was and I told them no. He was afraid how normal I was going to be when or if I survived, even after the MRI and doctors assuring him they found nothing.

My son would tell me later while they were waiting, he had begun to write my eulogy. He was planning to speak at my funeral and was deciding what music to play. I have always joked with my family about making sure Gary Puckett sings at my funeral. He was picking out the songs.

My daughter-in-law shared with me about one of the trauma doctors had walked through the waiting area on his way to refill his coffee. He stopped and asked if they were the patient's family. He was sorry to hear about what had happened. My son shared with me he told them they needed to be prepared because I would not make it. When they explained the doctors were still working on me, he couldn't believe I was still alive.

Being moved to the rehabilitation wing also meant I had to do more than just lie in bed all day. The doctors and nurses set goals for me each day. To sit on the side of the bed for a short time, move to a chair when I ate my meals and manage to eat more of my meal, which proved to be almost impossible. My body had taken a huge hit, killing all the natural bacteria in my stomach.

Everything I ate not only tasted the same, but made its way straight through me.

Because of the breathing tube being in so long and the medications I was given, my taste buds were not working correctly. I tried almost everything on the hospital menu, but everything had the same nasty taste.

I was beginning to think it was the hospital food, which always gets a bad rap until my husband brought in some cashews for a snack. I love cashews, but when he gave me one, it tasted just like the hospital food. I realized then I was going to have to eat whether it tasted good or not.

Feeling bad I couldn't find anything that tasted right, my husband raided the hospital refrigerator one night. He found an orange Creamsicle. It had to be the best thing I had eaten in the past two weeks. It wasn't on my diet, but the nurses didn't seem too upset when we told them. The threat of a feeding tube lingered over my head for the rest of the week. I needed more calories in my diet. The nurses tried to convince me to drink the protein drinks which were offered on my menu. They tasted awful. I can't imagine anyone finding these drinks good, but I'm sure they are good for you.

Being moved to the rehab floor also meant I could have visitors. No one other than my family over ten years of age were allowed in ICU. My first visitors were my granddaughters Alexa and Alivia, dressed in their Halloween costumes. Alexa was Dorothy from the Wizard of Oz and Alivia was Minnie Mouse. My other granddaughter, Kara, also came to see me.

My second visitor was one of my friends, Natalie. Her first question after me sharing what I knew of what had happened to me with the help of my husband filling in blanks was if I was going to give up control of things in my life. I laughed because I knew exactly what she meant. I never realized how much I tried to control each situation until I had to give up control of every simple function of my life and depend on other people.

My next visitor was my good friend and writing partner, Maggie. She had to see for herself I was all right. The look on her face when she saw me was priceless. It was as if she couldn't believe it was me. She was in charge of updating all my writing friends about my condition, asking for prayers and passing messages back and forth. Maggie and I met when I attended the romance writing course she taught through the adult education program. She seemed to have a lot of connections and drive, so I became a stalker. I joined all the writing groups she suggested and went to conferences she suggested. We soon became friends and now we write together with one of Maggie's childhood friends, Glenna, as The Stiletto Girls. I can't imagine my life without her. I consider her not just a friend, but family.

This was her Facebook post that day:

*UPDATE ON C. DEANNE ROWE: I saw her, I saw her, I saw her with my own two eyes! She's doing better, but not out of the woods yet. She's still drugged, but she did recognize me. She had physical therapy today so was tired. I was only in the room with her for about two minutes. Her son was there and snuck me in.*

She brought me my Christmas present early because she felt I needed it more at this time than at Christmas. It was a beautiful necklace with a stiletto charm. Along with the necklace was a journal and pen so I could begin writing down thoughts and not forget. I've made good use of these. During one of our conversations after I was home, I was telling Maggie about how my life had changed and her response was 'write it down'. She knew I was looking for the answer to why this happened. Her thought was the reason all of this happened was so I could write about it. It would help me work through it. That's what we do. We write. I took her advice and began making notes about everything I could remember. I would piece them together later.

Of course, when Natalie and Maggie came to visit, I couldn't wait to tell them about being kidnapped and my visit from a Klingon. Everyone else I felt safe with, I shared the news about my visitor. Everyone's reaction was the same. They smiled and laughed and passed it off as the sedation I was under.

Another week of sitting up for meals, physical therapy, nurses taking blood, administering medication, taking my blood pressure, giving me breathing treatments, insulin shots and chest x-rays and checking my INR number would pass before I was able to be released. I had never heard of INR before. Having survived blood clots meant I needed to become familiar with what my INR number was. INR stands for International Normalized Ratio. An individual whose blood clots normally and who is not on anticoagulation should have an INR of approximately one. The higher your INR is, the longer it takes your blood to clot. In other words, as the INR increases above a given level, the risk of bleeding and bleeding-related events increases. On the other hand, as the INR decreases below a given level, the risk of clotting events increases. My INR needed to be above two.

After a discussion about sending me to a Rehabilitation Center close to my home until I could take care of myself was nixed, I was happy I was going home. My husband was able to take vacation time from work to be my caregiver again, so home is where I was going. Now I knew everything that had happened to me, I was also afraid to leave the hospital for fear it would happen again.

Even with the excitement of being home, not having nurses interrupt my sleep every few hours and being able to see my precious dog, the fear of the blood clots returning lingered.

# GOING HOME

They released me from the hospital on November
7th. The flowers I received filled the back of my Pilot. The
nurses would all make special trips to my room because
they had heard about how beautiful my flowers were.

They sent home me with a CPAP machine.
Monitoring my oxygen, the doctors had performed a
sleep study while I was in the hospital. The results
showed I stopped breathing thirty times a minute, which
meant the CPAP machine was necessary.

They also sent home me with a walker, which
proved much easier for me to maneuver around than
with the crutches I had been using since my knee
surgery. I would be more stable with a walker and it also
became a toy for my grandchildren when I wasn't using
it.

After lying flat in a hospital bed for almost two
weeks, I had lost all the muscle control I had gained
since my surgery. I had taken a backwards slide. All the
things I had been able to do for myself, I now needed
help. I thank God every day for my husband.

They assigned home health nurses and a physical
therapist to me and would come to my home to work

with me. For the next few weeks, I would see them at least twice a week. As scary as the thought of being home and not having nurses available at the push of a button was, I was not alone.

They made an appointment with my general physician within a few days of leaving the hospital, which meant I had to make a trip out of the house to her office. My husband managed to load me into the back seat of my car, which had been the way I traveled since my knee surgery. It was raining, and I was weak, so I was no help at all getting me in and out of the car. When we reached the doctor's office, my husband retrieved an available wheelchair and pushed me through the doors and then back to one of the exam rooms. I couldn't wait to tell the nurse, Barb, about her daughter being one nurse who took care of me in ICU. Barb explained how her daughter had kept her and my doctor informed of my condition. Barb told me they weren't supposed to do that, but they were really worried about me.

My doctor came into the room, said hello, gave me a hug and we both cried. I don't know for how long, but I remember it giving me a sense of certainty. Other than when my husband finally told me why I was in the hospital, I believe this was the moment when I finally realized how close I had been to dying and how grave the effects of my condition could have been. She had read my medical records and let me know how lucky I was I didn't have any ill effects. The fact I was alive was a miracle. Being able to walk, talk, and all my organs were functioning normally was another miracle. The concern mixed with relief was telling on her face.

I was given instructions in my hospital discharge papers on how to sign into the hospital's portal. I could check my appointments, send emails to my doctors to request appointments or if I had questions. I could also see the entries that had been made in my medical records. The first time I selected the tab to view my medical records, I couldn't believe what I found. One of the entries was labeled 'Deceased'. Everything that happened just became real. I was so shocked, I quickly closed the tab. I wish now I would have taken a screen shot or a picture. When I signed in again, the entry was labeled 'heart failure'.

I could also order copies of my medical records. I wanted to blame someone for all the trauma I had gone through. I had a medical attorney go through my records to make sure there was nothing inappropriate. He couldn't find anything. I had no one to blame. So why had this happened?

I have always fallen back on religion for help. Belief in God had gotten me through the tough times in my life. I had been baptized when I was a young girl and had re-dedicated my life to Jesus Christ when I was in high school. Religion always played a part in my life, but most of the time was idle until something came up in life when I needed it. This was one of those times when I desperately needed it. I prayed and praised God for my health and for being given another chance at life to spend with my husband and family. I knew he heard me. My fear of being home was made easier because I could feel him with me at night when I slept.

My husband moved a chair from the living room to our bedroom before my knee surgery. I was told I needed to change positions every hour or so to help keep blood clots from forming. The chair was close enough to my side of the bed I could manage moving to a sitting position without help. This chair is where Jesus sat with me, comforting me as I slept. I would wake around three o'clock every morning and be awake for several hours. During this time was when I would pray, or what I began to call this, was having conversations with God about my life and how things were going to change. Since my priorities had changed, I was re-examining my life. What was important and what wasn't.

What I needed to give up and what needed my attention. My health was the first on my list of priorities. I wanted to be around to spend time with my husband, family and to see my grandchildren grow up.

People began asking if they could come see me. I didn't feel like visitors, but I couldn't say no. I had been cooped up at home while I recovered from my knee surgery and now my recovery would be longer. I wanted to catch up on everything I had been missing. Taking a shower exhausted me, so having visitors wore me out. I was also trying to sort out everything that had happened. I realized everyone wanted to see me to make sure I was all right and to help in any way they could. I appreciated their concern, but they couldn't give me the answers to questions I was looking for.

A couple from my writing group stopped by to bring me a get-well card and also a gift card to one of my favorite restaurants. Another writing friend had made lasagna and another a casserole. My supervisor and two of my coworkers had stopped to bring me a gift and also let us know the department wanted to buy my family Thanksgiving dinner. They had collected money and all we had to do was select what we wanted and they would pay for it and we could pick it up when we were ready for it.

My husband is very selective about his Thanksgiving dinner. We still had to make his favorite. giblet gravy and cornbread stuffing. He was in charge of that. The rest was taken care of.

The Christmas holiday was coming soon. I had done no Christmas shopping for my family. Amazon loved me this year. Not having the strength to spend shopping at the mall, the shopping came to me. Taking a shower each day zapped any strength I had, so almost every gift given to my family this past Christmas came from Amazon.

I had been looking at laptops for several months.

I had decided I wanted an Apple Mac Book. The first Saturday after I came home from the hospital, I woke from a nap to find a plastic bag from Best Buy lying on the bed next to me. Inside was a new Apple Mac Book. My husband explained it was my Happy Birthday, Merry Christmas, Happy Mother's Day, Happy Anniversary and thanks for not dying on me present. Christmas shopping done on my new laptop via the internet helped me pass the time while I rested and healed.

Being left home alone only for short periods of time meant my mother and my hero dog that hardly ever left my side were there with me while my husband ran errands. Mom returned home after Thanksgiving, meaning I would be alone more often for longer periods of time. My home health nurse suggested a medic alert necklace. I could wear it twenty-four seven. In the shower or wherever else I was. If I needed help, I just pushed the button. If I collapsed like before, help would be sent if I couldn't or didn't answer the operators. I never thought I would be the wearer of one of these, but I did feel better when I was alone. They are worth the money if for nothing more than a sense of security. Merry Christmas to me.

# CHILDHOOD MEMORIES
## *My exposure to religion*

Before I share with you another day in my life,
which will be with me forever, I want you to understand
the role religion played in my life growing up. Going
back through my experiences as a child has helped put
into perspective on how this event affected my life.

Growing up, religion was always a part of my life.
Saying prayers before eating, going to sleep each night,
and attending church on Sunday was normal. My
paternal grandfather had read the bible cover to cover at
least three times before I was in high school and my
grandmother was volunteering at their church whenever
she was needed, funerals, weddings, celebrations of any
kind. Neither one of my grandparents knew how to drive
a car. They walked everywhere they went. Living directly
across the street from their church, it seemed my
grandmother was at the church every time the doors
were open.

Some of my earliest memories are ones spent with
my sister, Becky and I running around the church while
our grandmother helped in the church kitchen. During
one visit, my sister and I made our way to the sanctuary

where there was a large wooden box in front of the Altar. We were curious, so we climbed and peaked inside the box. I remember my sister telling me we had to be quiet because the man's eyes were closed and he was sleeping. We had never experienced a funeral before, so we did not know this was a deceased person in a casket. I remember my grandmother not being very happy with us. She kept a closer eye on us from that day on.

My mother shared the story of her baptism with me. She was baptized when she was ten years old after attending Vacation Bible School. The preacher would talk to the kids every day about Jesus. My mother and one of her sisters became Christians. She shared her newfound faith with the rest of her family and, as a result, her mother, who was another faith, and her father, who did not go to church, were baptized. I didn't know this story until I was older and my mother shared with me. I never thought to ask either set of my grandparents how they had come to know the Lord. I assumed their experience had been like mine, raised in a religious family who taught them to believe.

When my grandfather passed, the church he belonged to etched his name on the front glass doors in memory of him. Even though he was only a member of the congregation and not a member of the clergy, he still greeted each person as they walked through the doors.

For as long as I can remember, there was a portrait of Jesus Christ hanging on my grandparent's living room wall. All my life, when I thought about what Jesus looked like, this portrait came to mind. I also had received a wooden bible holder from my Sunday school teacher for learning the most bible verses during our study of Paul, which I still display proudly on my bookshelves. The same image of Jesus was on the front.

As I got older, my family's attendance at church dwindled. I would attend church occasionally when I was old enough to drive myself.

Like most people, life consumed me. Between a husband, children, and work, I felt I did the best I could with the time I was given. I loved my family and if asked, I would tell you they knew how much I loved them and what they meant to me. I would be wrong.

The most regret I have as a mother is not giving my children the same exposure to religion as I had. They grew up knowing about God and Jesus, but I wanted them to be able to choose how they believed. I wanted them to be exposed to different religions and their beliefs because as I child I remember believing God was a loving God but also being afraid because you could also go to hell for breaking the commandments. I was taught not to play cards on Sunday, not to dance and not to curse. As a small child, I feared God and the power he wielded. I didn't want my children to be afraid of religion. I wanted them to be curious about religion.

I finally learned God doesn't use his power to intimidate or make his followers fearful. For every event in your life, good or bad, he is right beside you, walking through the fire with you, holding your hand.

I now know how much easier my life would have been in the past had I recognized the presence of God in my life in every situation, big or small.

There are a few times I realize I had a guardian angel. One time was when my maternal grandfather passed away. I was in high school. I had a dream he passed a week before he actually did. This was the first time death had so closely touched my life. The thought of never seeing him again was almost too much to bear. I visited his grave. I went alone so I could have a conversation with him. I approached his gravesite in tears when an overwhelming feeling of peace overcame me. It was as if he was with me. I could hear his voice telling me not to be sad. I didn't need to come back here. He wasn't there. He was in heaven with his Savior.

I needed to go live my life. He would be with me wherever I was. I would never be without him. I drove away and never returned until my grandmother's funeral.

Another experience was driving to visit my mother and father. My husband was out of town on business. I was eight months pregnant with our first child. My husband and I lived in the panhandle of Texas and my parents lived in southwest Oklahoma. I started out on my trip with what I thought was a full tank of gas. We had made this drive several times, and I knew I could make it without stopping if my tank was full. There is a stretch of road which is nothing but prairie, tumbleweeds, and tarantulas. Before you begin this long drive, there is one gas station, then nothingness. I glanced down at the gauge to see how I was doing with gas and my tank still read full. I knew something was not right and the gas station was coming up, so I pulled in. At this time, the attendants still pumped gas for you. When the attendant collected my money, he commented on it was good I stopped because my tank was almost empty. I don't want to think about what all could have happened if I had run out of gas on the long stretch of road.

The third experience was when I was receiving radiation treatments for breast cancer. My husband faithfully drove me to treatment every day for six weeks, but he had to stay in the waiting area while I received my treatment in another area. I told him how lonely it was while I was waiting for the technician to come get me. There were a few people in the patient waiting area and I kept noticing familiar faces each time. One woman in particular stood out to me. We started talking. We realized we had had surgery on the same day, Friday the thirteenth, and now we were receiving radiation treatments at the same time. Sharing with each other became a way to pass time. One thing we never exchanged was our names. It never really seemed important. We saw each other every day. The day of her last treatment, she presented me with a gold and pink angel pin. Another breast cancer patient had given it to her with the instructions to pass it along. I thanked her and then realized I didn't know her name. She told me her name was LaDonna. I had to choke back tears when I told her that was my maternal grandmother's name. I realized then all this time I hadn't been alone.

There are so many times in my life things have happened which can only be explained as a gift from

God. I'm sure everyone has those times when you know for a fact what just happened was a miracle.

We don't get to choose our path in life. It is already decided for us. I remember as a small child being told every hair on our heads is counted. God has a plan for all of us. All we have to do is trust and believe God will work for the good.

It doesn't matter what church you attend, what denomination you are, what color your skin, if you believe you shouldn't play cards on Sunday or dance. A church's doctrine is only a way to reach God. I pray every one finds a church whose leaders believe and share a message that helps bring them closer to God. God's plan is God's plan. We just have to decide if we bring God along for the ride or let him drive.

Now that you have an idea how religion played a part in my life, I'll share with you the other day, which changed my life forever.

DECEMBER 19, 2015

This is a day I will remember along with October 23, 2015, because of the life altering events of these days.

My husband had prepared lunch. I made my way from the bedroom to the kitchen table. It was laundry day, so my husband was in and out of the laundry room right off the kitchen. I hadn't thought about what he was watching on television until the show caught my attention. It was as if one particular scene had frozen on the screen.

My husband returned to the kitchen table and noticed tears streaming down my face. Of course, he asked what was wrong now. Since my surgery, my emotions had been everywhere. I have always been able to cry at the smallest things, but now it was almost every day. Television commercials, birthday cards, you name it.

I pointed to the television and with my voice cracking, I explained, "That's my Klingon".

My husband took a seat in his chair as he told me he was watching a documentary titled 'Jesus, the lost 40 days'. He explained the image of Jesus was a 3-D reproduction taken from the marks on the Shroud of Turin. He reminded me he had tried to tell me when I was in the hospital the man in my room was an angel, but I was insistent he was a Klingon.

I couldn't say anything. I ate my soup, letting the moment sink in. It seemed I couldn't control my thoughts. So many things were running through my mind. This would be the first of many pieces of the puzzle explaining what happened to me. I didn't just die six times in the ER that day. I was taken to the gates of Heaven and Jesus comforted me there. He gave me a choice to go with him or to stay. As He listened to my heart, he could feel the despair and sadness at the thought of me leaving my husband, kids and grandkids. He let me return with the knowledge I and everything in my life would be all right.

I also realized a few weeks later that He called me Deanne. When I was in the hospital, the doctors and nurses called me Carla, unless they were corrected by my family, because that is my legal first name. Only Jesus would know.

****

My husband was the only one I told about what had happened. The next day, we attended church with my son and daughter-in-law to watch our granddaughter's Christmas program. With my thoughts still trying to understand what had been revealed to me, I had planned to tell my son then, but the time was never right.

That night I sent him a text telling him everything and even including a picture I had found on the internet of the image the documentary had used of Jesus. I wasn't sure the response I would receive. To my joy, he believed me. He was amazed at the power of Jesus. He told me he had no words, but it made sense. I was down, sad and vulnerable and Jesus made sure I understood by showing the documentary and making sure I watched it. One thing he said that stuck with me and was 'He is real'. I knew then everything had happened to me for a reason.

A few months later, as we shared more about my experience, I told my son and daughter-in-law about feeling Jesus sitting with me at night in the chair next to my bed when I first came home from the hospital. My daughter-in-law's eyes filled with tears as she told me she had prayed for Jesus to let me know he was with me. Now she and I both knew her prayers were answered.

I know my family is having as difficult a time dealing with what happened as I am. The difference is my family thought they were going to lose me, but I survived. I died, and by the grace of God, I was brought back to life. I know how precious life is and how it can be taken from you in a split second. I also know what waits for us when we die. I'm no longer afraid of death.

There was a strange period of grieving afterward. Everyone was saying you should return to normal, but I learned there is no normal. I have to process what happened to me and learn to make it part of my life going forward. I'm in the process of searching for my new normal. With God's help and counseling, I'll eventually find it.

## LIFE AFTER TRAGEDY

When my father passed away in 2000, I walked around in a fog for several months. Something about losing a special person in your life takes away the laughter and the enjoyment of everyday life. Realizing you won't ever talk to or see this person again in your lifetime here on earth is life altering. When losing someone close to you, there are other people around to help you rejoin life. You can pick up the pieces where you left off and learn to live your life again. My father lived in a different state, so my everyday life changed little. The only change was knowing I could never pick up the phone and call him. I would think of him, then remember he was gone.

When you suffer a tragedy or trauma like I did, rejoining life can prove to be very difficult. It is impossible to pick up the pieces where you left off before the tragedy. Those pieces don't fit any longer.

My family and friends rallied around me after my trauma to make sure I was healing and regaining my strength. As time passed, those people went back to living life as they knew it and I felt left behind. I'm still trying to find where I belong and my new normal. My priorities have changed.

I returned to work and life trying to resume my responsibilities as I knew them before I left for my surgery. I realized people had stepped up to cover for me not only in life but at work while I was recovering. I appreciated everything everyone had done. I expected when I returned to work, my co-workers would be happy to see me back so things could return to the way they were before I left. I could begin taking care of my share of responsibilities. I was so wrong.

The atmosphere in my department was cold and quiet. I finally concluded that past saying hello and welcome back, people didn't know what to say to me, so they didn't. A coworker who had taken some of my responsibilities while I was out on disability was promised changes to her position by her boss in return for her work, which didn't happen because I returned to work. I had stolen her glory. I ruined all the accolades she had received while I was out. She wouldn't talk to me unless she had to and then it was always rude and demeaning. I soon realized she would have been happy if I had not returned.

Returning to work meant I had to rejoin life. It was one of the most difficult things I had to do. I was not physically or mentally prepared for what I was returning to. My position is not only stressful but required me to sit for long periods of time, which is one thing people who have suffered with blood clots shouldn't do. I wish I could say I was happy to be back, but I would be lying. I was not only fighting to readjust to my life, I was also fighting to readjust to a workplace which seemed so familiar but had completely changed.

My daughter did her best to convince me I should change jobs or retire. Make a new start. I couldn't talk about it without tearing up. There were so many nights I came home from work, crawled into bed, and cried myself to sleep.

The day I returned to work was one of the worst days I had experienced since my collapse. I had spent the day trouble shooting because my computer had crashed while I was out. Also, my work cell phone on which I receive work emails and text messages wasn't working because my network password had expired and I couldn't change it from my laptop or cell phone. After working with our help desk, I could sign back on the network and then change the password on my work cell phone. I had several text messages, which I had missed while my phone was out of commission. One of those texts was from my daughter. This is what she wrote:

*Mom, I just wanted to let you know a few things. Things I have really just kept to myself as I've watched you recover. First, I hope you know how proud I am of you. You keep fighting and fighting and you don't give up. Second, words cannot express the joy I feel every day that we still have you with us and I don't foresee that joy diminishing for me anytime soon. I'm sorry I haven't been with you much this week, but I know I've been with you in spirit. I love you very much and I'll see you tomorrow no matter what!*

I can't tell you how much I needed that message, especially on that day. I've learned that when God puts an obstacle in my path, he also gives me a miracle to help me through. This was the miracle I desperately needed. I wrote her back telling her I had just seen her message and explained why. I thanked her for being there for me. I loved her too.

Her reply back was she didn't mean to send the message to my work cell phone, but she guessed it was meant for me to read it later. She was so right.

When talking to my daughter-in-law, she gave me a suggestion which turned out to be one of the best ones I was given. She told me to pray for the people at work. I listened to her suggestion, but I had to toss this idea around for a while. The thought of praying for the person who was blatantly rude to me was almost as difficult for me as it was returning to work. I did it though. Every night I say a quick prayer for everyone and especially this unhappy co-worker, and I still do. I keep telling myself Jesus had told me he would take care of me. I hold on tightly to those words.

I won't say things got better immediately. My supervisor and my boss made me feel welcome and told me how happy they were to have me back. They were glad things could return to normal. They had no idea how far this was from the truth and how normal was no longer normal.

I armed myself by placing a small carved wooden cross my mother gave me when she was visiting in the pocket of my purse. I remember her telling me she carried it with her all the time and how it made her feel better. Praise God for another miracle worked in my life.

I'm still doing my best to rejoin life. I'm watching my family resume living, slowing giving me space and not feeling as if they have to fuss over me. I have to admit, I miss them fussing over me. I find myself wanting more time with them because I know how precious our time is, but I also know I have to let them build memories in their lives with their families.

I'm also returning to some of the things I loved to do before my experience. I recently attended a writing retreat with people from my writers' group. The last writing retreat began on the day I collapsed and ended up in ICU, so attending this one was crossing another fear off my list.

My friend, Maggie, was sick and unable to attend the retreat, which gave me cause to rethink attending myself. Her support would have made it easier for me to be there. I decided to go. I needed to begin finding my way again and trusting I would be fine.

I'll never forget what happened to me, but I think it will get easier to look forward to life instead of trying to decide where I belong or what I'm supposed to be accomplishing. I still have a hard time listening to people complain and worry about what life is handing them. I do my best to stay quiet when I would love to tell them how menial these events are. In the grand scheme of things, these things just don't matter. I want to tell them Jesus is real. I've seen him. He comforted me. If they trusted God with their lives, things would be so different. They don't have to worry or fret. There is such a peace in knowing they have someone to walk with them through all their trials and tribulations. Telling my story could be the way I accomplish this.

I know there will be people who don't believe what I'm writing, but I also know there will be people who do. If just one person learns to believe from my story, it will have all been worthwhile.

## ONE YEAR LATER

It has been almost a year since my knee replacement surgery and just short of a year since I died. I still have so many questions that I don't have the answer to. I'm finding out more and more each day. I wanted to know how everyone found out about what happened to me. My husband has told me what he remembers several times. He works downtown, so he rode the bus to work this day, which was a normal thing. When my mother called him, a cab was sent for him and he was taken to his truck and then had to drive back downtown to the hospital where I had requested to be taken. He thought to stop by the house where he collected my glasses, my computer and basic necessities. He still did not know what condition I was in. All he knew was I collapsed and was taken by ambulance to the hospital. He had talked to the EMTs as they worked on me. They told him they thought I was suffering from COPD. He insisted if it was anything, I had blood clots. Somehow, he just knew. It wasn't until he reached the hospital, he found out I coded as soon as I reached the hospital. As he walked up to the Hospital, one chaplain greeted him from the hospital staff. They asked if he was here for Carla. He knew then it wouldn't be good news. It wasn't very long ago he confessed he had not been able to ride the bus to work since that day.

For my son's birthday, he didn't want presents. Instead, I purchased journals and gave one to my son, daughter and daughter-in-law so they could write what they remember about that day. I thought a lot of my questions would be answered when I read them and I could include some of their memories in this. I'm still waiting to receive the journals. Hopefully, I'll receive them before I finish this story so some or all can be included.

I recently had an appointment with another of the doctors who treated me when I was in ICU. This was the doctor that packed and unpacked my nose to stop the bleeding. He remembered me, but when I told him I didn't remember him, he reminded me I was asleep for the packing. The unpacking was another story. I remember that vividly. We also discovered at some time during my trauma there were two holes placed in my nose, one in the cartilage which separates the nostrils and the other in the nasal septum. I don't know what can be done about this, but it will have to wait until I'm off blood thinners.

Another issue I had a deal with was my hair falling out. I thought it was because of the blood thinners I was taking. I read that was one of the side effects of blood thinners. After some online research, I found out around three months after your body has suffered stress and trauma, your hair would begin failing out. There would be hair all over the bathroom counter where I would get ready every morning. My husband and I would have to clean my hair from the roller on the vacuum cleaner each time we ran it.

I also had my last appointment with the counselor I have been seeing. When my husband and I decided I needed to seek counseling, we called several counseling services, and they put my name on a list. They wanted to check my insurance company to make sure my insurance would cover my sessions. I didn't hear back for several months. I never realized how difficult it was to find counseling. I didn't push because my time was occupied with physical therapy and doctor appointments. I finally did some additional research and emailed this therapist, desperate for someone to talk to. She made an appointment with me right away. She would worry about my insurance later. She was another miracle.

I was terrified to talk to a professional about what I had experienced, but I knew I needed to. Not only was I terrified, but I was also apprehensive about what to discuss with her. I had never been to any type of counselor before. It was unfamiliar territory for me. I quickly learned she would be a lifeline for me with no judgment or criticism.

Her office was simple. A leather couch against one wall, a desk angled in front of a large window, a single chair across from the couch which she would sit in during our sessions, a lot of children's toys and a book shelf filled with her collection of Pez dispensers. I learned after several sessions she and her mother had both been on blood thinners. We had a connection.

During our sessions, she listened while I talked. The first few sessions I cried, and she patiently waited and when I managed to talk, she listened. It wasn't until the last few sessions I was able to get through our sessions without crying.

We talked about a lot of things but mostly my difficulty trying to rejoin life and return to work. She and I agreed I finally have a handle on the changes I had faced and the ones I will be facing in the future. I hope we are right. I plan to stick around for a long while. God willing.

I summoned the courage to tour the Trauma Center and Critical Care Unit where I spent a week of my life completely helpless, dependent on nurses and doctors for my every need. The first several days they kept me alive. I had a deep desire to know what this place, which was so important to me and my existence, looked like. I remember little of anything about the trauma center. I only remember one room in the Critical Care Unit, which I never got a chance to see completely. My only view of this room was lying flat on my back and one short period sitting in the chair next to my bed. I learned I was in room fifteen for an entire week. Most of that week, I didn't really know or care where I was. I could have been in a bungalow on a sandy beach and would never have known the difference. During my visit, I made sure to leave a note for my favorite nurse. Since he wasn't working that day, I didn't want to miss the chance to let him know how much I appreciated and was thankful for everything he did for me during my stay. I pray it made him smile when he read it.

I recently had appointments with doctors I haven't seen since before I suffered my trauma, my OBGYN and the surgeon who performed my breast cancer surgery. I was given a long hug from my surgeon's nurse, Kim, in the exam room after she learned what happened, and another hug as I was leaving. Everyone one who learned about what happened to me said the same. I am a walking miracle. People who suffered the same double pulmonary embolisms as I did don't survive. The same thing the nurse told my son the first night I was in ICU.

I have had long conversations with God and devoured every article or book I can find on near-death experiences hoping to come up with answers to questions I have. I realize each person's experience is different. Now that I have experienced something I had only heard about, was interested in but never imagined would happen to me. What am I supposed to do with this knowledge? Also, what am I supposed to do with my life? I've been told so many times how I was saved for a reason. I was brought back because I have a purpose, something I haven't finished. I have spent the past six or seven months trying to understand everything completely. Analyzing and remembering everything, every minute and every second.

I know this experience has changed me, my thinking, my beliefs and my everyday existence. I keep falling back on the reassuring words I was told, "You have to fight, Deanne. We'll take care of you". I thought that only applied to when I was recovering in the hospital. I am also finding out it applies to my everyday life from then on. I'm banking on the fact I have someone who will take care of me until we meet again.

Until that time, I'm doing my best to try and live an everyday existence. I watch people who complain about the smallest things, whose life is totally turned upside down by some small thing someone said or did.

I have to admit, that was me before. I cared what people thought of me. I cared how I looked and acted around people who would judge me for the smallest imperfection. Those days are gone. I've learned to say 'no' to everyone's demand and not care what everyone thinks or says.

But with this newfound acceptance of myself comes confusion about how I'm supposed to act. I sit in meetings, which before I would participate. Now I have a hard time caring about anything that is said or discussed because I know in the grand scheme of things, they don't matter. I also find off-hand remarks concerning death or dying have a big impact on me. Where I might have laughed before or let someone's comment slide, now I find this subject difficult and affects me in a way I never expected.

I recently read an interesting article stating people who had near-death experiences have left well-paying jobs and prestigious careers for opportunities to help others and be of service to people in need. I completely understand their thinking. I've given serious thought to leaving my job since my experience to try and find something more satisfying and fulfilling. Something with which I could change people's lives.

No one on earth knows where this experience will take me. I just wish I could give everyone reading this the knowledge that I have acquired. The existence of unconditional love of a higher power to me, known as God. Someone who I no longer pray to like I did before, but have conversations with. Not just when I am in need, but every moment of my day and night. I learned God is with me at all times, knowing every movement and thought I have. I depend on him for every second of my existence.

These past months have been especially difficult, so my conversations with God have been plentiful. As I attempt to return to a routine of work and life, I'm having trouble keeping a positive attitude. Don't get me wrong, I realize how lucky I am to wake each morning. Before I walked through each day with blinders to what life was really like and how the difficulties we face each day affect us. Now they are like flashing red lights beckoning me to pay attention. I have yet learned how to turn them off and I'm not sure if I want to. I do become overwhelmed and my reaction is to retreat to a safe place and shut everything out.

There are still a few things which bring back memories of that day in full force. Friday mornings are one because that was the day of the week I collapsed. I also avoid my husband's side of our bed because that's where I collapsed. My heart beats faster and I feel very unsure each time I'm there. I look at the floor and wonder how I fell. Where did my legs go? How did I fit between the nightstand and the window? How was I lying when they found me? I don't linger long.

The chair my husband moved next to my side of the bed is still there. I've been wanting to move it back to the living room, but it brought me such a sense of security when I first came home from the hospital. I feel if I move it somehow, I'll hinder my recovery. This fear is one I would love to conquer.

The next pages are messages I have received from friends and family telling their memories from this time. I included them, as they made me realize I was not the only one whose life was permanently altered.

# MAGGIE'S MEMORIES

All I can remember about Oct 23 is sitting around the conference table at the hotel (writing retreat) and Ryan letting me know you were in the hospital ICU and not doing well. Time stopped. Breathing stopped. Thinking stopped. Not sure what my expression showed, but the room erupted into what's wrong? What's the matter? Etc. It seemed like an eternity passed – everything was in slow motion. I remember thinking I really needed some air. I remember shaking as if I were freezing to death and I remember tears. Eventually I got words out of my mouth. "It's Dee." To me another eternity passed by before I could say, "Something's wrong. She's in ICU." At some point, I must have breathed because my lungs stopped hurting so bad. Eventually it seemed as though my brain caught up with my thoughts and I could tell the rest you were in ICU from a blood clot, and you were stable at that point. Ryan kept me posted with texts as often as he could. Visitors weren't allowed and I couldn't see you. All I could do was rely on Ryan.

Sleeping the next few days was non-existent until my body finally said it was exhausted enough. Then I could sleep for a few hours at a time. I kept dreaming they were trying to take you away from me. I don't have a sister. But, if I did, it would have been you. To me, it felt like my sister was in that hospital bed and they wouldn't let me see her. I had to see with my own eyes that you were there and that you were okay.

When Ryan told me you could have visitors, I headed to the hospital as soon as I could get off work. I saw Ryan when I stepped off the elevators. Bless his little heart for being there. It was easier walking into your room with him walking with me. He told me he had just stepped out because you were sleeping but I could take a peek at you.

You were slightly asleep but stirred when we walked in. You looked like hell but you were the most beautiful sight to me. A huge relief flooded over me and, of course, tears wet my eyes and probably my face as well but I really don't remember. All I do remember is just how beautiful you were laying there looking like hell warmed over.

I don't think I was there more than five minutes. Didn't want to take a chance on tiring you or causing you any kind of a problem. My steps leaving were much lighter than when I walked into the hospital. I stepped onto the elevator and leaned against the wall shaking with the sobs that I could finally release. I got off the elevator and started down the hallway, still racked with sobs and I remember thinking, as I passed by people, that they were going to think I had just lost a relative or something but I really didn't care. I was just so relieved.

As I walked and cried, I saw a gentleman walking toward me and when he got close, he held out his arms and I walked into them. He stood there and let me cry as he hugged me. He never said anything – just let me cry. Finally, I stepped back and said thank you. He said, "You're welcome. Sometimes we just need a strong shoulder to cry on." He went his way, and I continued on mine.

Ryan continued to let me know how you were doing and finally that you were going home. That was a happy day and yet a scary day, too. I probably had all the same thoughts you did. All the "what if's." It was scary, but I knew you were in good hands – Craig's and God's. I knew that in time, my "sister" would be okay. Not "normal," not back to her "old" self or even her "new" self but okay. Just okay, because that's what I had asked for. Okay to be alive, okay to be her old self, okay to be her new self and okay to be.

# MY FAMILY'S MEMORIES
## MOM

I flew out of Memphis on Tuesday night for Des Moines. Craig and Deanne picked me up at the airport and we went out to dinner. Wednesday Deanne had a physical therapy session and Thursday Deanne and I had a good day visiting. Catching up on everything happening in our lives.

Friday morning, I woke up to the dog barking upstairs. She kept barking so I went up to see if she needed to go outside. I tried to open the back door but couldn't figure out how to open it. I went to Deanne's room to ask her how to open the door and that's when I found Deanne on the floor between the bed and chest. She must have tried to get to the phone before she fell.

I saw she was stressed. I started to scream at her to tell me what was wrong. She told me to call 911 and I did. I didn't remember the house number or street but Deanne had given all the information to Smart911 a few weeks before. They knew right where we were and were on their way.

I asked Deanne for Craig's number and called him. He said to call 911 and I told him that I already had called. The paramedics came in soon after and worked with Deanne, but they lost her once while they were trying to get her into the ambulance. They were able to revive her and head to the ER. Craig called and talked with them and agreed to meet them at ER.

I remember shouting to God that he had brought Lazarus out of the tomb, and he now needed to save Deanne. Sara came by and picked me up on her way to the hospital. When we arrived, the doctors told us that Deanne had flat-lined three times while in the ER. She was unconscious for two days, and finally when she awoke we went in and I put my hand on hers and she gave it a squeeze.

# BROTHER AND SISTERS
## Mike and Lisa

When Lisa and I found out you were having knee replacement surgery we were both uneasy about it and I think that was normal reaction. The only thing was that the more we talked about it the more my medical training kicked in.

I had been in the operating room during these procedures and I knew the good and the bad. You know all doctors and personnel are taught to give worst case scenario first then benefits.

Well, worst case scenario kicked in and I couldn't get it out of my head. I didn't want to put that out there. When I got the call about your problem, I felt powerless and fearful for what you were going through. Love you Sis.

## Becky

Most everything I knew during this time came from Mom even though I did talk to you and Craig several times. Conversations were short and not much information was exchanged other than you were feeling all right. There were continued prayers for your recovery and, once Mom returned home, she had lots of questions about what happened. She was extremely emotional and couldn't talk about things in detail.

I remember being concerned when she told me you were having trouble writing, organizing your thoughts. I know this is your way of processing – dealing – creating. I was very troubled by that. I am so happy that you are choosing this venue to try to understand. It is your comfort zone and will see you to healing. I will be praying you will find what you need through your efforts. Please take a moment to realize that there are people that might be blessed by what you have been through and may be inspired by your story. Love you.

# AUTHOR'S FINAL THOUGHTS - 2018

I wish I could say I have found my new normal and moved on with my life learning from my experience and applying what I've learned to each new day. I'm still searching. I know I will never be able to return to life as it existed before this experience. I have to take a new path which I'm still trying to find. I've encountered many forks in the road. Depression being one of them. I thought I had beaten it, but it returned with a new vengeance. I never know when I wake in the morning if I'm going to smile or cry, if I have the strength to get out of bed and face the day or cover my head and hide from what seems an unconquerable force.

I've started seeing a therapist again. When I recognized the symptoms of depression coming on, I sought out help. First from my doctor which we decided together I needed medication to help. I don't like having to be medicated to face each day, but as it began to work, I realized it helped me in so many ways. The benefits outweighed my objection.

On October 13th, my son, Ryan, sent me a text message after he had arrived at work. He had started a new job a little over a month before, which required him to drive downtown past the hospital where I was taken. His text said:

*The worst part about working where I work now is I have to drive by Methodist every day. Days of driving in the rain and days like today where I see an ambulance rushing to save someone gives me flashbacks. Momentarily, I have the fear, sadness and numbness wash over me again. But, it's more and more being replaced with hope, sublime faith, and a smile that you are still here to see all of us grow a little more every day. I'm sorry that you had to go through what you did, but I just wanted to let you know that your resolve and strength are now a fabric within my soul. I'm sorry to drop this on you during a workday and in text but I was moved to say something. I hope you enjoy your Friday.*

*I love you more than anything, Mom!*

This is the reason I chose to return. My husband, my children and grandchildren. I know all of us have been changed forever by what happened. The people and priorities in my life are continually changing. I've learned to let people and things go that don't belong. I also realize how many people God placed in my path to help me survive and deal with my experience. I believe these are the most precious things I have learned from my experience. Knowing what and who are important to you and your purpose in life is priceless. Knowing you don't have to please everyone who crosses your path. You have to learn to let go and ignore people whose objective is to spread their negativity to you and cling to the ones who strengthen you. Also, it's all right to say 'No'.

I know people are wondering why I wrote this. Why I didn't just let my experiences go, find my new normal and begin living my life again. The answer is simple. I can't. There is something inside of me telling me I need to share my experience. Putting this together has helped me process what happened. It is helping me work through everything that happened and come out on the other side. No matter how much I learn about what I went through, I don't want to forget a single second.

Each additional day I'm given, I want to learn to wake up and realize how lucky I am. It might take me a while longer to accept my experience as the blessing it is, but I'm on my way. All I can ask from my family, friends, and from anyone reading my story is to pray. Pray for me, pray for your family, pray for your friends and anyone who might pass through your life. I promise you I will do the same in my conversations with God.

# REFERENCES:

Page 1
Serenity Prayer
Reinhold Niebuhr (1892-1971)

Lord, grant me the serenity to accept the things I cannot change, courage to change the things I can and the wisdom to know the difference. *

Page 11

John 11: 1-44, The 6TH Sign: The Resurrection of Lazarus.

When Jesus appeared before the tomb where Lazarus had been placed for three days, he called in a loud voice, "Lazarus come out". The dead man came out, his hands and feet wrapped with strips of linen and a cloth around his face. Jesus said to the people, "Take off the grave clothes and let him go".

Page 18
Caringbridge – www.caringbridge.org

Free Websites That Keep Family & Friends Connected During Health Events.
Easy to Start & Manage · Create A Free Website · Safe, Private & Ad-Free

Types: Compassion, Donation, Connection

## PRAYER OF COMFORT

Psalm 121:5-8King James Version (KJV)

[5] The Lord is thy keeper: The Lord is thy shade upon thy right hand.

[6] The sun shall not smite thee by day, nor the moon by night.

[7] The Lord shall preserve thee from all evil: he shall preserve thy soul.

[8] The Lord shall preserve thy going out and thy coming in from this time forth, and even for evermore.

According to the National Blood Clot Alliance (www.stoptheclot.org) On Average, 274 people die every day from Blood clots. On average, one person dies every six minutes from a blood clot. Understands the risks. Know the signs and symptoms.

Pulmonary embolism: Take measures to lower your risk - https://www.mayoclinic.org/diseases-conditions/pulmonary-embolism/.../syc-2035464...

Pulmonary embolism occurs when a clump of material, most often a blood clot, gets wedged into an artery in your lungs. These blood clots most commonly come from the deep veins of your legs. This condition is known as deep vein thrombosis (DVT).

Signs and symptoms of pulmonary embolism (PE) include unexplained shortness of breath, problems breathing, chest pain, coughing, or coughing up blood. An arrhythmia (irregular heartbeat) also may suggest that you have PE. Sometimes the only signs and symptoms are related to deep vein thrombosis (DVT). Jul 1, 2011

Pulmonary embolism is fatal if left untreated. Blood clots can break off and move into the lungs heart and brain depriving the body of the oxygen and blood supply that it needs and causing permanent tissue damage and death. However, if caught early, a blood clot and a pulmonary embolism are extremely treatable.

*What does a blood clot in your lung mean?*
A pulmonary embolism is a blood clot that occurs in the lungs. It can damage part of the lung due to restricted blood flow, decrease oxygen levels in the blood, and affect other organs as well. Large or multiple blood clots can be fatal. The blockage can be life-threatening.

*What does it feel like when you have a pulmonary embolism?*
It is due to a blockage in a blood vessel in the lungs. A pulmonary embolism (PE) can cause symptoms such as chest pain or breathlessness but may have no symptoms and be hard to detect. ... PE usually happens due to an underlying blood clot in the leg - deep vein thrombosis (DVT).

*How do you get rid of a pulmonary embolism?*
Aggressive treatment may include thrombolytic medicines, which can dissolve a blood clot quickly but also increase the risk of severe bleeding. Another option for life-threatening, large pulmonary embolism is to remove the clot. This is called an embolectomy.

*Can you recover from a blood clot in the lung?*
Blood clots in the lung can sometimes cause left-over symptoms of shortness of breath, decreased exercise ability, or chest discomfort, but most people recover completely. However, in a few patients, clots do not completely dissolve and significant chronic damage to the lung results, called pulmonary hypertension

*What is the survival rate of a pulmonary embolism?*
Patients with PE who received mechanical ventilation, cardiopulmonary resuscitation, and thrombolytic treatment had very high mortality rates of 80, 77 and 30% respectively. However, patients stable enough for diagnostic procedures as Spiral CTs and V/Q-Scans had mortality rates of 1 to 2%. Sep 30, 2002

*Pulmonary Embolism.* Having a blood clot in the deep vein of your leg and having a previous pulmonary embolism are the two greatest risk factors for pulmonary embolism. For more information on risk factors for blood clots in the legs, see the topic Deep Vein Thrombosis.

Practical Steps to Keep DVT Risk Low
- Ask your doctor about need for "blood thinners" or compression stockings to prevent clots, whenever you go to the hospital
- Lose weight, if you are overweight
- Stay active
- Exercise regularly; walking is fine
- Avoid long periods of staying still
  - Get up and move around at least every hour whenever you travel on a plane, train, or bus, particularly if the trip is longer than 4 hours.
  - Do heel toe exercises or circle your feet if you cannot move around
  - Stop at least every two hours when you drive, and get out and move around
  - Drink a lot of water and wear loose fitted clothing when you travel
  - Talk to your doctor about your risk of clotting whenever you take hormones, whether for birth

control or replacement therapy, or during and right after any pregnancy

- Follow any self-care measures to keep heart failure, diabetes, or any other health issues as stable as possible
- Know the symptoms of DVT and PE symptoms and signs of Deep Vein

Thrombosis (blood clot in the leg)

- Swelling
- Leg pain or tenderness
- Reddish or bluish skin discoloration
- Leg warm to touch

## C. DEANNE ROWE

C. Deanne Rowe was born and raised in southwest Oklahoma. She has also lived in Nebraska, Texas, and California. Iowa has been her home for over thirty years where she lives with her husband, two children and their spouses, five grandchildren, and her hero teacup toy poodle, Allie.

She has always loved writing poetry and short stories and became a published romance author later in life. She has published thirteen books of her own, three in her *Valley Series*, six in her *Cowboy Temptation Series*, three in her Puckerbrush series and one non-fiction, Comforted From Heaven. As one of the Stiletto Girls, she is an author of eleven novellas in the *Stiletto Girls Series*. Learn more about C. Deanne Rowe, her books, sign up for her newsletter, and receive a free ebook at:

www.cdeannerowe.com

Made in United States
Orlando, FL
11 August 2023

35974556R00078